I0488334

# Scribble Lika Boss

Steevo Tapia

KingSA

ISBN-10:0692416943
ISBN-13:978-0692416945

# DEDICATION

Dedicated to the man who made me the man I am today my Pops-David Tapia
RIP June 28, 1955-April 28, 2015

# CONTENTS

## ACKNOWLEDGMENTS

I want to thank everyone who has inspired me in many ways to pursue my collection of Art Scribble pads. For all the inspired artist who continue to be creative and present all your masterpieces for the world to enjoy! My hopes are to inspire the inspired. Thanks.

KingSA

KingSA

KingSA

KingSA

KingSA

KingSA

KingSA

KingSA

KingSA

KingSA

KingSA

KingSA

KingSA

KingSA

KingSA

KingSA

KingSA

KingSA

KingSA

KingSA

KingSA

KingSA

KingSA

KingSA

KingSA

KingSA

KingSA

KingSA

KingSA

KingSA

KingSA

KingSA

KingSA

KingSA

KingSA

KingSA

KingSA

KingSA

KingSA

KingSA

KingSA

KingSA

KingSA

www.ingramcontent.com/pod-product-compliance
Lightning Source LLC
Chambersburg PA
CBHW040742200526
45159CB00023B/1590